Overcoming Fear

The Ultimate Cure Guide to Build Confidence to Destroy all kinds of Fears (Criticism, Failure, Death, Flying, Public Speaking, Darkness, Heights, Spiders......)

David .O. Joseph

No part of this publication may be reproduced, or transmitted in any form or by any means including photocopying, recording or other electronics or mechanical method without the prior permission of the publisher except for brief quotations embodied in critical reviews.

Copyright © 2018 David O.J

ISBN: 9781720172918

Table of Contents

Preface

Do you know that mental infection and disorder can be cured the same way we cure body infection? Fear of all kinds and sizes is a form of psychological infection affecting both your physical and mental health. Fear can last for a brief moment and then pass, but it can also last much longer, and you can get stuck with the situation. In some cases, it can overwhelm you and take over your life, affecting your ability to live peacefully and enjoy life. You will find it difficult to sleep, eat, concentrate, travel, or socialize. Fear can hold you back from doing things you want or need to do, and also affects your physical condition. If your fear is causing distressing thoughts or feelings, be reassured that you can get better with proper management

This book will help you on how to overcome your fears, anxieties, and worries for the rest of your life. You need to realize that by facing your fears you are not trying to master the art of closing your eyes to danger but to identify the threat, understand it and then overcome it with utmost courage. Once you can determine the cause of your fear, then you can look into various options that will help you conquer the fears and be able to live a healthy life. Here you will learn about causes of fear and anxieties, what happens in your brain when you are afraid, how to choose the right foods that can drastically cut down on the amount of anxiety you experience. The book also shares **ten points action plan** that will help you to build **CONFIDENCE** and destroy your fear.

Incorporate these ten points **(CONFIDENCE)** into your everyday life and see your fears melting away in record time.

You will be able to

C- Challenge to conquer; **O**- Obey to control; **N**-Nourish to flourish;

F-Fight to win............. and **E**- Exercise to victory

1. Introduction

Fear is an intense emotion that can override all other feelings, logic or priorities. It can lead us to act out of nervousness, frustration and sometimes anger. Similarly, when our actions are founded on fear, we almost always make poor judgments and decisions which can have undesired consequences for us and our relationship with others. Fear is the principal enemy of success; it diminishes hope, hinders progress and annihilates billion of dreams. Most fear is mainly psychological. Panics, worry, tension and other forms of mental disorders are products of negative imagination. Stephen Melish called fear an idea-crippling, experience-crushing, success-stalling inhibitor inflicted by no one but you! Different opinions have been given about fear, and the irreducible conclusion is that fear is an illusion inexistent in the physical world. It exists only in our minds and manifests through our actions. It is an affliction we architect gradually that subtly develops into a monster dictating the tempo of our lives. No wonder Seneca stated, "We are more frightened than hurt, and we suffer more from imagination than from reality."

Fear can last for a brief moment and then pass, but it can also last much longer, and you can get stuck with the situation. In some cases, it can overwhelm you and take over your life, affecting your ability to live peacefully and enjoy life.

You will find it difficult to sleep, eat, concentrate, travel, or socialize. Fear can hold you back from doing things you want or need to do, and also affects your physical condition.

To conquer fear, we must understand the following related terms Imagination, Illusion, and Minds. They are what you should know and have a deep and clear-cut perceptive.

What is Fear?

Fear is a feeling induced by perceived danger or threat that occurs in certain types of organisms which causes a change in metabolic and organ functions and ultimately a change in behavior such as fleeing, hiding, or freezing from perceived traumatic events. (Wikipedia)

Anxiety

Anxiety is a word we use for some types of fear it is an unpleasant state of mental uneasiness, nervousness, apprehension, and obsession. It is a natural human reaction to traumatic and stressful situations but becomes an issue when it turns out to be nagging and persists without a trigger. It has to do with the thought of a threat or something going wrong in the future, rather than right now. The American Psychological Association (APA) defines anxiety as "an emotion characterized by feelings of tension, worried thoughts and physical changes like increased blood pressure."

Mind

The mind is a set of cognitive faculties including consciousness, perception, thinking, judgment, and memory. It is usually defined as the faculty of an entity's thoughts and consciousness. It is also responsible for processing feelings and emotions, resulting in attitudes and actions.

Imagination and illusion

An illusion is an act of manipulating the mind to see what actually doesn't exist as a reality. In other words, an illusion is a distortion of senses, revealing how the human brain normally organizes and interprets sensory stimulation. Illusions may occur with any of the senses, but visual illusions (optical Illusions) are best known and understood.

Illusion can be used to explain fear because they actually don't exist in the real world. You are the architect! Only you can see, feel, hear them, and perhaps, someone subjected to the same circumstance.

Imagination is the image-making power of the mind.

Those ghosts you saw when you were young, those voices under the bed, where are they from?

Although fear can be stressful and crippling, it plays a crucial role in our lives. We would live with reckless abandon if we are not aware of the notion

of fear, taking unhealthy risks, and performing all sorts of downright hazardous activities. The most important thing is the ability to distinguish between actions which provoke a healthy acknowledgement of apprehension against unreasonable triggers of fear which impose an unnecessary limit and hinder our progress. Being fearless means knowing how to leverage fear it doesn't mean eliminating it.

Is fear innate or learned?

Some fears are instinctive; some are learned and while some are taught. Pain, for example, causes fear impulsively because of its effects. We learn from past experiences to be afraid of certain people, places, or situations because of negative associations. For example, a near-drowning experience may cause fear any time you move near a body of water. Other fears are taught: in some places, societal norms often dictate whether something should be feared or not. People will be warned of the consequences of violating certain norms to avoid a particular thing or face a consequence that cannot be logically explained.

2. What Happens In Our Brain when we are Afraid

The brain is the starting point of everything we sense, do, and think. ¬It is a complex organ with more than 100 billion nerve cells comprising an intricate network of communications. These cells are continually transferring information and triggering responses to put our body in survival mode during the fear attack. The brain response to fear is almost entirely instantaneous as we don't consciously prompt the process or even know what's going on until it has run its course.

Fear begins with a frightening stimulus and ends with the release of chemicals from our body system to prepare the body for defense. It works this way: something frightens you, like hearing a sudden loud noise, seeing a snake along the yard, or feeling a sudden bite in your body. You become panic and anxious. You experience certain physical reactions such as rapid heart rate, increased blood pressure, tightening of muscles, goose pimples, sharpened or redirected senses and increased sweating. Your body goes into fight-or-flight mode, ready to do everything possible to make you safe.

Research has discovered that certain parts of the brain play central roles in the process.

Thalamus

This is a small structure within the brain placed just above the brain stem between the cerebral cortex and the midbrain and has extensive nerve connections to both. The main function of the thalamus is to relay incoming sensory signals (from sense organs: ears, eyes, mouth, skin) to the cerebral cortex.

Sensory cortex

The sensory cortex is located in the frontal lobe of the brain. It receives all sensory input from the body and generates neural impulses that control the execution of movement.

Hippocampus

The hippocampus is located in the medial temporal lobe of the brain. It stores and retrieves conscious memories; processes sets of stimuli to establish context.

Amygdale

The amygdala is highly involved with different emotional responses; in particular, it detects fear and prepares for emergency events. It decodes emotions; determines possible danger and stores fear memories.

Hypothalamus

The hypothalamus is a small area in the center of the brain with many functions. It plays a crucial role in hormone production and helps to stimulate many important processes in the body. It activates a "fight or flight" response.

The Impact of Fear

Our body is planned to respond quickly to fear by sending out powerful hormones and signals to various body systems to give the energy needed to run or the power to struggle for survival. But when the fear impulse goes awry, and coping mechanisms become unmanageable it results in a disorder that causes us to feel the side effects of fear even when there is nothing to fear. It impacts our mental and physical wellbeing, leaving us susceptible to intense emotions and impulsive reactions.   Here   are   some   ways apprehension creates chaos in our life and impacts those around us.

Physical health

Fear weakens our immune system causing our body to be unable to move or to move only with wobbly knees. It can cause cardiovascular damage, irritable bowel syndrome, and decreased fertility. According to the University of Minnesota, fear can also have long-term consequences on our health, including "fatigue, chronic depression, accelerated ageing and even premature death.

Brain processing and reactivity

Fear can disrupt some process in our brain functions that allow us to control emotions, read non-verbal cues and interpret data presented to us. To someone in chronic fear, the world looks scary, and their actions confirm that. Fear can weaken the creation of long-term memories and damage the hippocampus, short-circuiting the response paths and be causing constant feelings of anxiety.

Mental Health

Untamed fear can have a genuine impact on your daily functioning and quality of life. Depending on the level, you might find it a real struggle to run errands, travel or even make it work every day. It can also make you experience social isolation, which can contribute to you becoming reclusive and depressed. In other words, it can considerably impair your education, your career, and your overall quality of life.

Similarly untamed fear can make you feel helplessness. When you realize how your fear has affected several or even all aspects of your life, like your career, social life, and general happiness. You may feel that the situation is out of control and become discouraged about life.

3. Understanding Fear and Anxiety.

Fear and anxiety are interrelated as they often occur together. Some see them as indistinguishable while others perceive them as a distinct phenomenon. When faced with fear, we often experience the physical reactions that are described under anxiety. They often cause similar symptoms, such as increased heart rate, shortness of breath and tensed muscle as a result of the body's flight-or-fight instinct.

Anxiety is a generalized response to an unknown threat or internal conflict, whereas fear is focused on known external danger.It is understood that fear triggers defensive behaviors in animals. They may flee or do anything just to escape the presence of the danger. Defensive behavior cannot be triggered if the danger is not identified visually or at least, felt. This is opposed to anxiety, as the danger is not defined. It is mostly down to curiosity and sometimes, confusion. You are anxious about something because you don't know what will happen. If you do, you don't know when it will happen, how, or why, whereas, your quizzical mind wants to see the future or find answers to the questions, such as "how am I going to cope?", "will this speech be approved tomorrow?"

The difference between anxiety and fear is that unlike people experiencing fear, symptoms leading to anxiety occur even though there is no apparent risk or cause of danger. But in most cases, the reason the individual feels anxious cannot be identified. This is in stark contrast to fear, where the individual can readily determine the cause of the fear.

The bottom line is that anxiety has no specific danger or threatening situation. It is the future, perhaps, future in the next thirty seconds intimidating someone from the present. If you know what you are particularly afraid of, and you find it threatening, based on what you believe or how you fared the last time a similar situation came and was traumatic. It is fear. Fear is more external than anxiety. The danger might only exist in your own world; (others cannot feel what you are feeling.) but it is present and imminent to you. People suffering from anxiety often find themselves powerless and unable to cope with their symptoms to such an extent that it begins to influence their daily activities and relations with people. Anxiety is often one of the main causes of other emotional disorders, such as depression and nervous tension.

Fear, on the other hand, can often make an individual become empowered to face the problem. Once you can determine the cause of your fear, then you can look into various options that will help you conquer the fears and be able to live a normal life. What is causing the confusion between anxiety and fear is that they are often used together with the ever-present conjunction, "and." If they are the same, it will mean that fear is synonymous with anxiety, and anxiety, to fear. It surely does not make sense to utter a statement like, "it was easy to differentiate and distinguish." The conjunction, "or" will be and more appropriate conjunction there, so, anxiety may be viewed as a more pronounced or elaborate form of fear, which provides individuals with an

increased capacity to adapt and work towards bettering the future.

"Anxiety is a unique and coherent-affective structure within our defensive and motivational system" Barlow. Anxiety is built on fear, but fear is not built on, nor around anxiety. It is easier finding your way around anxiety than fear.

Fear Completely Untamed: Phobia

A phobia is a form of mental illness in the form of anxiety, defined by a persistent fear of an object or situation. It automatically repels the affected individual, as he will go to the farthest extreme or the greatest lengths to escape the situation or object; typically the actual level of danger is exaggerated in the mind of the victim. If the feared object or situation cannot be avoided, the affected person will be troubled to the highest order. We can also define a phobia as an extreme or irrational fear of or aversion to something.

4. Getting Up! Turning Back to Face Your Fear

The earlier part of this book has gone far beyond being succinct in explaining fear and anxiety. Scientific explanations and how our mind entertains fear were made clear. The causes, the circumstances that trigger us to flinch when the intimidating circumstances arise were critically explained. Definitely, you must be aware of your triggers. You may/may not be mindful of what hindrance it has been posing. This is why we have to examine Jack Canfield's words, "Everything you want is on the other side of fear."

It should be clearly understood that you are not trying to master the art of closing your eyes to danger but to identify the danger understand it and then face and overcome your fears with utmost courage, ensuring that the sense of danger will not set limits to your greatness. You will instead embrace it and navigate your path to the end of the tunnel.

Resilience comes from facing your fears - facing your fears will help you in creating enormous success. It is the only way to beat them. Avoiding them doesn't make them go away. You will become better than your environment and transform yourself above the fear. Resilience starts with you, and it begins in your mind.

Fears help you decide what's real.

When you take the time actually to challenge your fears, you will be able to Separate necessary concerns from baseless worries and confront what scares you head-on. You learn to separate fact from fiction. The chances are that some things you're afraid of will be valid while many will be mental worst-case scenarios that have been amplified in your mind than they ever will or would in reality

I've had a lot of worries in my life, most of which never happened. - -Mark Twain

Fears enrich you and help you develop compassion.

Dealing with fears helps you to be compassionate. When you yourself have gone through the situation, you will understand better. You will be able to show and feel compassion toward others experiencing similar situations. You can put yourself in the shoes of someone who is just starting, and that empathy can help guide that person to fight fearlessly to overcome the situation with greater zeal

Nelson Mandela, one of the great men and heritage of Africa pointed out, "I learned that courage was not the absence of fear, but the triumph over it. The brave man is not the man who does not feel afraid, but he who CONQUERS that fear."

Mark Twain's perspective on fear and courage was similar to this view.

"Courage is resistance to fear, mastery of fear, not absence of fear."

Are you ready to resist?

Are you ready to grow into a full master of your fears?

Firstly, ask yourself, "What am I afraid of?"

I am sure it won't take a long time before you figure it out within you. The answer is always at the back of your mind.

Perhaps, yours is that you are afraid of heights?

Okay. Let's say you are afraid of heights just as an example. You have singled out what frightens you.

In the real sense of it, Heights are dangerous. Of course, your mind will warn you about the danger, (naturally) but this fear is preventing you from taking a roller coaster ride with your loved ones the last time you visited an amusement park on holidays?

This should not be. The warning is just to create awareness of danger, not to send you away. Overcoming the fear of heights is not tantamount to preparing to be a cliff-diver, (at least, not the primary goal) but you just have to TURN BACK! Ask your inner mind why you are afraid of it. You will realize that there is no genuine reason for it. It might just be simply,

"Because I am afraid of it." Notwithstanding, it is high time you progressed. It is time to grow, fight and survive.

Denial is powerless.

Negligence is never helpful!

Transform your mind and expunge anxiety!

A lot of energies are trapped within the human body. Most of these are being inappropriately utilized. We need to learn to channel our energies to the right path so we can become our better selves. This is part of what transforming an anxious mind does to you. From experiences and from what we have learned, we all have stress, anxiety, and fear in our lives. It has deprived us of sleep and peaceful nights, made some of our days excruciatingly unbearable and in the long run, making life less lively and enjoyable.

Perhaps, your anxiety and fear are built around work, family, school, social life, love life, and what have you. This transformation plan is still required to re-orientate you and your inner compass. Calming the mind by deeply relaxing can help transform and make the mind and body an old tough bird, never broken, always soaring. Too many of us are not living our dreams because we are living in our fears-Les

Brown. Are you living your dreams or fear has taken everything?

As explained earlier, anxiety is that feeling of worry, nervousness and unease which swiftly and steadily sweep away your confidence, sound mind and well-being. An aggravated situation of this may lead to depression which is compounded by regret over failure and limitations.

The Transformation protocol

Meditate and ruminate.

Amit ray stated that if one wants to be victorious over the anxiety of life, one has to dwell at the moment or other words, live in the present. Meditation is a simple exercise of the mind which anyone can pull off. It is simply being calm and placing your focus on a particular subject. You may just decide to sit calmly for some minutes in a day. Follow your breath, say and repeat positive words under your breath. During this time, ensure that you observe your thoughts, feelings, believes, emotions, sensations with compassion without judgment. You may practice this in the early hours of your day, before other activities come calling and also, later in the day or in the evening will do. Ten or five minutes long medication is sufficient and healthy for your mind. Make sure you meditate, ruminate and reflect on what makes you afraid.

Guided visualization

Visualization exercise is helpful and necessary in this case. Examine the things that always bothered you or things you are anxious about, and then take a few breaths. Center yourself and relax completely after. Since our minds are capable of untold imaginative power, (which is part of what breeds our anxieties and fears) why not channel the creative mind to visualize positive things about the future? See the fear and incessant anxiousness feasting on your dreams and well-being approaching an abrupt end.

Harness the power of a positive mindset and imagination. Your thoughts got you into this trouble; they are very much available to lead you out. Alas! An entrance is always an exit at the same time. Remind yourself that you can handle whatever you are facing and chose to get back to a peaceful state of mind." Nothing can bring you peace but yourself"- Ralph Waldo Emerson.See anxiety as a message from your unconscious mind that you have an event in your life or future that MAY end in a negative way. Underline the word, MAY. It does not have to end in a negative way, does it?

Get nourished to flourish. Are you the type that is of a habit of skipping breakfast for no reason other than you being busy?

Are you a fan of excessive sugar consumption, processed foods, or grabbing a drink or two later in the evening? You may be inadvertently contributing to your anxiety every day by eating foods that create anxiety symptoms while avoiding foods that may fight anxiety. The truth is that your diet does matter. What you eat affects your mood, and how you feel. It stands to reason that changing your diet to one that is made for those living with anxiety can be a valuable part of treating your anxiety symptoms. Help your mind and body with what you take in. Chapter seven tells us what to eat to stay healthy.

Logic, reasoning and conceptualizing

Ensure you train your mind to view things from the better perspective. Remind yourself to be as realistic as possible too. Be attentive to what your mind tells you about any feeling or experience. It may be different from what really is. Is it ever true? Can it be ever true? Utilize logic and reasoning to examine the validity of thoughts that stroll into your mind. Seize control and learn to filter your thoughts. And remember, we must first accept our present lot if we wish to have a different encounter or experience in the next moment.

5. How to Build Confidence to Conquer Fear

Although the role of fear is to keep us safe, you do yourselves no favor by living in fear. To awaken your potential and draw in more significant possibilities, you must eradicate fear from your lives through daily efforts which promote our strength and self-security. Shying away, overlooking or ignoring your fears is a fruitless effort and inappropriate way of dealing with the situation. It is like stuffing an unpowered refrigerator. When you open, you are met with an unpleasant odor which will make you close the fridge hurriedly. However, closing the refrigerator will only bring temporary relief; it will not eliminate the offensive odor. As long as the dirty stuff is not removed the smell will persist when you open. Of course, there are some fears that we think are not really consequential to the way we live. For instance, if a person has a fear of facing a crowd, or public speaking apprehension, and he or she does not deem it as a big deal because he has no intention of facing any crowd, talk less of addressing it. There is really no motivation or need to work on conquering it because it has no immediate value. If fear is fast becoming a stumbling block that will disallow you to do the next big thing in your career/life, beware! It is time to fight and snap out of it.

Conquering fears start with the acknowledgement that oftentimes fears is a choice, not a fundamental trait that cannot be subdued. Incorporate these 10 proven strategies (CONFIDENCE) into your everyday life and see your fears melt away. Applying them might be the touch of golden you are craving for.

How to Develop the CONFIDENCE to conquer fear

C - Challenge to conquer. Challenge your fear. Separate necessary concerns from baseless worries and confront what scares you head-on. The chances are that many of your qualms are superfluous in the greater scheme of your life. When you face tough problems don't stay mired in the mud behaving like a drowning man, take action. Take a deep breath and challenge your fear right before it grips you. What is the worst that could happen? Ask defiantly, and you will probably see that the worst you are afraid could happen will not, as they are most likely to be the products of your imagination.

O- Obey your intuition to take control. Intuition consists of ideas that come to the brain naturally. Intuition allows you to go deeper into yourself and makes you more effective in your activities and happier in your relationship. When things aren't going well or when you need to react quickly to a situation, it is your intuition that guild you and makes you adapt much better to your environment.

Intuition is a powerful tool when it comes to making an essential decision in your life; following our intuition is the simplest way to live. It can guild us to the right pathway of life and help us to become the person we are destined to be. Speaking and acting in keeping with intuition naturally bring more joy, personal satisfaction, and peace of mind.

N – Nourish your body and soul to flourish. Healthy eating can really make a big difference in facing fear. Changing your diet to one that is made for those living with anxiety makes a great deal of sense. Eating diets rich in fruits and vegetables can keep your anxious moment in check. Furthermore, staying away from unhealthy burgers really will help improve your situation and well being. You will learn more in Chapter 6 of this book about how healthy eating can minimize anxiety situation.

F – Fight fearlessly to win. Fear exists, but it is conquerable. Note that fear of all kind and sizes are physical and psychological infection mental disorder. Develop self-confidence and fight fearlessly. Change your mind set. Fear stems from not believing enough in your own abilities and talents. To shun fear forever, you have to work on your personal self-worth. When you consistently put down yourself and live in the mindset of "I can't do it" or, "I'm not good enough," you narrow your chance of success and inadvertently limit your progress.

I - Isolate to suppress. Identify the underlying factors of your fear. Isolate them and take action. Doing nothing about a situation strengthens fear. You are not in complete control of your emotions, but you can have it suppressed, and so doing, dictate how it affects you. If you have to cry, let it out through those tears, but come back stronger to fight again and again, till the last drop of sweat dries off. Embrace your environment also, so you will devise a proper battle plan to fight for what you want. This is not a piece of advice to partake in violent acts, but teaching the mindset of insisting on achieving success. It always comes with a price to pay, and a prize to keep in the end. Live strong! Die-hard!

D – Destroy to overcome. Fear can be the buildup of too much stress. A busy life with too many schedules results in fear of failure. It's crucial that you take time out for yourself to calm down, relax, meditate and alleviate your anxieties. So calm down, take a breath and destroy all the negative and doubtful thoughts and focus only on the things that will bring joy and motivation. Eliminate your negative thoughts before they become mental monster troubling you, destroy the negative imprints and move on. Learn to always focus on the good side of your experiences and do away with the bad feelings. There is always something to be grateful for in our lives, regardless of how difficult our situation. Self-appraisal is when you give compliments and celebrate yourself. Celebrate those little victories or triumphs that do not matter. Revel in the good moments and victories, instead of bothering way too much on the unpleasant side of life. Praise yourself, but do it within you most times. It is never tantamount to being arrogant and unrealistic.

E - Embrace change to replenish. Change your mindset and perception. Some

People are afraid of change and will do anything to oppose it. Their concern is that change will somehow disrupt their lives or dislodge them from their comfort zone. But change actually works to carry us into new greater manifestations of ourselves. Therefore, tolerate important changes in your life, even if they may seem scary and terrifying at first.

N - Nullify failure to succeed. By understanding failure, you dig deeper into the actual meaning of failure. You have to realize that not being successful at something is not the end of it all. There is always an opportunity for a 'next shot' just that it might not come easy like before or on a platter of gold. Great minds, great scientists and renowned successful people in business or any career all have that unpalatable side of their story. This is when they are faced with a major setback in their endeavors. They never sat back, wailing and whining. Instead, they remain optimistic and restart. Failure is just a stepping stone to success; it is just telling you to make another attempt. Try another way around it. Move on and grow stronger.

C – Collaborate to prevail. Collaborate with people that matter. Learn from people and their experiences. When you have done your possible bests, and you are still having problems with fear, you don't have to face your challenges alone. You can source for help from people that can assist. Involve others such as a counselor, mental health Professionals, and spiritual leaders. Reach out, read relevant books, magazines, and journals. You may opt-in for documentaries and movies that can help you understand fear and anxiety better. Take note in your diary thoughts going through your mind. Write what you know, think or believe that scares and unsettles your mind. Connect them to what you have learned or experienced.

Also, prayer can help. Pray for guidance on how to overcome that specific fear. Pray for courage. Prayer is similar to meditation. You may choose to meditate, and by doing so, you are equipping your mind with a beneficial asset. It is a dosage for mental strength. You can also consult spiritual leaders as they may offer counsel and reassurance to give you a better understanding of the situation in the spiritual sense. When you need to express your mind to someone they are just there for you. They can help you learn ways and techniques to regulate your fear solve problems and control stress. A health-care provider can give you a physical examination and recommend relaxation techniques which can help you to manage the condition. Also, he may prescribe medications which can help bring the situation under control. He can also help you learn ways to express your feelings through role-playing and other methods.

E - Exercise for victory. Daily physical exercise protects the body against the effects of mental stress. Exercise improves mood. Working out can help you feel better. Physical exercise stimulates various brain chemicals that may leave you feeling better-off and more relaxed. There are different forms of activities that are relevant to different types of people. Some choose early morning joggings; some prefer the evening, some may just visit the gym, while some will join a dancing class. Whatever will get you sweating without the need for the application of mental or intellectual energy can bring about nourishment to the body for higher motivation.

6 Dealing with Common Fears

If your fear is causing distressing thoughts or feelings, be reassured that you can get better with proper management. Acting appropriately will help you to reduce the adverse effects. Here we shall examine some basic fears in a human mind and explain the ways of dealing with them.

Fear of Loss of Love

Lack of trust is the main reason for fear of loss of love in a relationship. The habits of cheating, lack of tolerance, perpetual lying, and disbelief are some vital factors causing the fear of loss of love. The best way of eliminating loss of love fears to build trust in the relationship. Those in the relationship should trust and respect for each other to maintain a healthy relationship.

Loneliness

The fear of being alone is related to doing something with no one noticing. It is caused by the lack of interaction with another human being. You feel abandoned, ignored, unloved, and unsatisfied with yourself. Thinking that for our actions to be meaningful, people must notice. Ordinarily, there is nothing wrong with being alone, but if it bothers you, you have to take some proactive measure to address the issue. The first step is to prepare to face the fear. Relax, and be happy with yourself, have the confidence that you will be able to manage to be alone. Try and look for activities that you enjoy that involve others. This will make you happy and will increase your chances of interacting with people. Furthermore, you can see a specialist. They can serve as a guide through the journey. Therapy provides a safe avenue for you to explore and continue to overcome the cause of the fear.

Fear of Death

Death remains to be the ultimate reality and continues to worry most people. You should understand that thinking about

death always is harmful to your health. With the constant fear of death, one may never be able to enjoy life. Dreading the future always deprives us of the present joys. Death is quite a natural phenomenon. Changing our thought pattern and behavior helps us eliminate the fear of death.

The Fear of the Unknown

The fear of the unknown has been with the human for thousands of years, and it is an excellent component of what has helped us survive as a species. The fear can be easily explained like this: your mind tells you that to move forward, you must know what is waiting there for you. You seem to feel that you need to know ahead to control the situation and that if you don't know, then you are at a loss. This fear of the unknown is the number one enemy of progress. We find it difficult to take risks, discover and understand new things. You have to Change your mindset and perception to conquer this fear. Closed-mindedness cannot help, be ready to leave your comfort zone and explore new territories. Change may be an instrument of transformation working to carry us into new greater manifestations of ourselves.

Fear of Criticism

The fear of criticism is one of the basic fears that are among people. It manifests in the form of tepidness, fear of conversation, shifting of eyes, lack of poise, and lack of self-confidence. The best way of eradicating this fear is by trying to accept criticism in the right spirit. Consider criticism as a way of betterment and work on your weaknesses. Take it positively and use it in improving yourself.

Fear of Darkness

Known as Nyctophobia, the fear of darkness is one of the most common fears that affect people. Symptoms include rapid breathing, irregular heart rate, sweating, and nausea. Fear of darkness is

often associated with negativity; it influences one's lifestyle and also affects those around him. To deal with this fear effectively, you have to identify its causes and overcome the reasons why darkness scares your mind. There are drugs which can help in alleviating the fear of darkness.

Fear of Flying

Fear of flying ranks among the peoples deepest fears. This might be due to unpleasant news of occasional air disaster. You overcome the fear by merely disabusing your mind. The fact that air transportation is part of our life is enough to give us safety assurance. Try to find out more about flying; you will see that it is the safest means of transportation.

Fear of Height

The fear of height could be as a result of early traumatic experience. If you suffer from the fear of height, there can be psychological treatment. There are several drugs and therapies also that can help you overcome the problem. Face the fear; consider the consequence of any actual harm resulting from the situation. Gradually expose yourself to a greater height.

Fear of Spider

Some people become anxious at the sight of a spider. You can overcome the fear by thinking differently about it. Dispel common myths about a spider and stop seeing it as a scary insect. Changing your perceptions about it is crucial to overcoming your fear. Get some facts about spider behavior. They are almost everywhere and often time unavoidable. They are usually harmless and would not usually attack anyone.

Fear of Public Speaking

The words 'public speaking' evokes fear and anxiety in the minds of most people. The average person ranks the fear of public speaking higher than the fear of death. Although the fear of public speaking is very real, you can overcome this fear when you realize the fact that speech giving is part of our daily living. We give a speech every day; at work, home or social events. When we are in a familiar place among peers, we are at ease in expressing ourselves. However, when the surrounding changes, our confidence level drops, but the good thing is that anybody can make a good presentation with adequate preparation and necessary techniques. When you organize all of your resources, it helps you to become much more focused, relaxed and calm.

7 Get Nourished to Flourish.

Some foods can help cure anxiety, and some can aggravate it. Choosing the right foods can drastically cut down on the amount of anxiety you experience – and possibly improve your condition.

Although anxiety isn't directly linked to diet, uncontrolled diet contributes to both the experience and the severity. Healthy eating leads to normal hormonal functioning, which leads to an improved sense of well-being. Certain foods provide essential vitamins and minerals that are known to relax the brain, calm the body, and increase the body energy. It stabilizes your mood and gives you the ability to think and act appropriately at all times.

Healthy eating can make a big difference. Eating diets with more vegetables and staying away from unhealthy burgers really will keep your anxiety in check. Therefore, changing your diet to one that is made for those living with anxiety when you suffer from it makes a great deal of sense. Then you can complement your anxiety diet with a useful treatment technique.

Here are some foods habits that may help ease you from feeling anxious all the time and increase your sense of well being.

Antioxidants Foods

Research evidence has connected anxiety symptoms with lower consumption of antioxidants. Antioxidant foods can quell anxious moods, relaxed your nerves, and protect the brain against oxidative stress. Foods High in antioxidants include carrots: Cranberries, blueberries, and blackberries, spinach, citrus fruits, red peppers, sweet potatoes, almonds, berries, avocado.

Water

Insufficient water in the body system always leads to dehydration. It can lead to your heart rate racing and make you feel light headed and dizzy; sensations that are common in panic attacks. Water has long been touted as an effective anxiety-reliever. Staying hydrated may reduce the feeling of anxiety and give your body a sense of freshness.

Tryptophan-Rich Foods

Foods rich in tryptophan contains natural relaxation component which calms your nerves and may increase your metabolism as well. It is known to induce peaceful sleep and regulate moods. Tryptophan is present in most protein-based foods. It is particularly plentiful in soy, chocolate, oats, dried dates, milk, nuts, seeds, beans, eggs others are yogurt, cottage cheese, red meat, and, almonds.

Magnesium Rich Foods

Magnesium plays a vital role in numerous processes within the body. It can help stave off the symptoms of anxiety as it is known to contain a calming mineral that has been found to induce relaxation. Magnesium may also act as a blood-brain barrier to check the entrance of stress hormones in the brain. Include Magnesium rich foods like green vegetables, black beans, nuts, seeds and avocado in your diet.

Omega-3 Fatty Acids

Omega-3 fatty acids contain all sorts of potential health benefits for your body and brain. It can fight depression, and anxiety studies have found that people who consume omega-3s regularly are less likely to be depressed and more importantly when people with depression or anxiety start taking omega-3 supplements, their conditions get better. They can be found naturally in fish, including salmon and tuna.

Healthy herbal teas

Herbal teas like chamomile Peppermint, Ginger, Hibiscus and Lemon are known to have various anti-oxidants properties that help in reducing depression and anxiety. Their anti-depressant properties help keep your brains calm and don't let your thoughts impede your actions.

Crucial Foods to Avoid

Avoiding the following foods can significantly transform your anxious mind. Preventing them is not likely to cure anxiety, but it will help in minimizing the effects. Remember, most foods can still be eaten in moderation, but healthier eating is still essential to healthy anxiety diet.

Fried Foods

Fried foods have little nutritional value and difficult to digest. It takes a longer time for your body to process and breaks down which contributes to heart struggles. It's not easy to reduce your anxiety if your body is poorly processing the food you consume.

Alcohol

Too much alcohol is not good for your body. It dehydrates your body and throws off your hormone and nutritional balance. It can cause you to do crazy things that create more anxiety in your life.

Coffee

Coffee creates a rapid heartbeat and some sensations that may create panic attacks. Also, excess coffee is a known anxiety stimulant. Ordinarily, if coffee is taken moderately, it may not be harmful to the body but the more you the drink, the more you increase the risk.

Acid Forming Foods

Acid creating foods like wine, yogurt, pickles, eggs and sour can drop magnesium levels in the body system. Low Magnesium level is a major cause of anxiety disorder in many of those suffering from anxiety symptoms. Therefore, cutting back on acid forming foods is important.

Dairy Products

Dairy products aren't inherently bad for you, but if you discover after consuming dairy products you feel more anxious, you have to decrease your intake. Excessive dairy products in the body can heighten your adrenaline levels and contribute to a more anxious state. Dairy products taking moderately is not bad for the body.

Refined Sugars

White sugar in desserts is not too good for your body. Fructose is not bad but sugar, like caffeine, stimulates your body in a way that can lead to nervousness that aggravates anxiety symptoms.

Conclusion

Fear creates stagnancy because it makes us to battle against ourselves and deprive us of the enjoyment in life. Excessive or relentless state of anxiety can have a devastating effect on our physical and mental health and those around us.

We do ourselves no favor by living in fear. We must eradicate fear from our lives to awaken our potential and strengthen our sense of well-being and self-security. Conquering fear will empower us for a richer and meaningful life. Only when fears are conquered can life be meaningful and lived in the real sense.

Overcoming Fear

About the Author

David has over 25 years professional experience working as a trainer, counselor, motivator, and administrator. He loves to help people change their lives and achieve their goals and objectives in life. David has written or edited a dozen of books where he shares practical techniques that anyone can use to make the desired changes in their lives.

www.ingramcontent.com/pod-product-compliance
Lightning Source LLC
Chambersburg PA
CBHW050047260726

48658CB00005B/1816